oke W

net Sauvignon

ONT'S

tore Rioja

Margaret River

y *The Douro*

Honeyed toasty bottle-developed Riesling, roasted pumpkin, brittle buttery sage, shavings of Gruyère ...

Crates of Cabernet Sauvignon **Larry Cherubino Wines** Franklin River

Dear Ceil
Happy Cooking!
Best wishes from
all your friends at
Apache Australia
x

Original 1980 Chardonnay plantings **Pierro** Margaret River

WINE
AND
FOOD

Roasted Kipflers, seared Wagyu, smoky paprika butter, youthful Shiraz, savoury tannins and dense spicy intensity …

Malbec grapes hand picked at **Cullen Wines** Margaret River

KATE LAMONT

WINE AND FOOD

PHOTOGRAPHY BY FRANCES ANDRIJICH

UWP
UWA PUBLISHING

CONTENTS

XI

INTRODUCTION

For me, matching wine and food comes down to flavour.

It's all about the 'weight' or intensity of flavour in the food and how that combines with the flavour of the wine. If either dominates, the experience will be less satisfying. My greatest pleasure as a chef is knowing that guests have enjoyed the entire food and wine experience rather than leaving with the memory of a particular wine or individual dish. That means I have done my job in creating true companionship of wine and food rather than just cooking a meal.

There are really just two basic ways to tweak or alter the intensity of flavour of any dish. One is the method of cooking, and the other is the combination of ingredients. So, for example, using the method of poaching will give you a very different finished taste from, say, roasting. Similarly if you use vinegar as an ingredient rather than lemon juice you still get a firming acidity, cleanliness and sharpness to the food, but the taste can be quite different.

A poached chicken breast topped with a fresh mango and mint salsa is a very different meal from a roast chicken with some herb and garlic butter tucked under the skin and served with roasted tomatoes. So, although chicken is the base ingredient of the meal, you would almost certainly serve different wines. The former cries out for a vibrant, zesty Riesling whereas the intense, rich flavours of the latter are all about ripe berry fruits, red wine with silky tannin, and lingering chocolatey flavours.

By understanding how to think about flavour and intensity in food you can make every dining opportunity more satisfying and glean greater enjoyment and value from your wine purchases.

When you are preparing food to serve with a specific wine either by variety or by age you may already have an idea of the wine's intensity of flavour. A rich, oaky, buttery Chardonnay would probably demand sturdy, densely flavoured food just as a young, peppery Shiraz would match a marinated barbecued lamb cutlet as opposed to a piece of grilled snapper. You could, however, by adding black olive tapenade, a rocket and parmesan salad and some home-cooked chips, create a fish meal that would be fabulous with the Shiraz.

It can be as simple as choosing to roast some pine nuts to toss through an avocado salad rather than tossing them in raw; adding a generous dollop of mustard to a

basic mayonnaise to build intensity of flavour; or frying some capers in browned butter to give them a toasty, caramelised taste.

The recipes that follow are simple, tasty and wine-friendly. Within each recipe you will see opportunities to tweak the flavours by using a timid or generous hand with seasoning and the flavour layering ingredients. You may choose to use salted (or preserved) lemon instead of fresh lemon. If so, you immediately change the robustness of the lemon flavour, which will allow you to serve, say, a Chardonnay or lighter-weight red whereas fresh lemon demands a more lively, aromatic unoaked white such as Sauvignon Blanc or Riesling.

A generous addition of anchovy, garlic and densely flavoured herbs like oregano and rosemary will give you a punchy salsa verde suitable for serving with a Pinot or a spicy Tempranillo whereas a subtle approach with soft herbs like basil and parsley and no anchovy will make a milder, gentler, less intrusive salsa verde more suitable for serving with Sauvignon Blanc or unwooded Chardonnay.

Of course there is no right and wrong; there are many great marriages, and we consistently see over the years as we experiment that marrying food and wine successfully is as much about the way we serve food as it is about the combinations of ingredients and flavours. When I was a teenager prunes wrapped in bacon were the pièce de résistance of sophisticated dinner parties; these days it may be fresh figs wrapped in pancetta. The underlying idea is the same; it is just that the way we choose to present those flavours has altered and evolved.

Many years of seeking to understand the companionship that creates a delicious dining experience in the simplest or most sophisticated occasion can develop an intuitive sense of what works and what doesn't. So practice makes perfect!

We've arranged this book in six chapters relative to flavour: subtle, light and restrained; and robust, substantive and intense. Of course you could tone down or beef up a recipe using seasoning and cooking technique.

There are chapters on dishes for white and red wines as well as Champagne and dessert wines. Each chapter then gives you specific recipes as well as ideas for specific wine varieties.

Thankfully we have moved on from white wine/white meat and red wine/red meat as our guideline and are beginning to revel in the accessibility of fresh ingredients, the abundance of passionate information about how to cook simply and effectively every day, and the adventurous nature of our wine industry, which seeks to produce wines of benchmark quality and value across variety and region.

The museum cellar at **Moss Wood** Wilyabrup

Barbecued crayfish
tails, kaffir lime
butter, a vibrant,
zesty, unsullied
new Riesling …

Dinner on the Dock **Lamont's** East Perth

1
CHAMPAGNE

It's all about celebration, flavour and taste.

Champagne is all about celebration, flavour and taste. For me the difference between French Champagne and Australian sparkling is the fabulous lingering aftertaste or 'length of flavour' you experience with the 'real' stuff. Vintage French is powerful, intense, rich and complex, and has a beautiful persistent bead (bubble). Non-Vintage (NV) Champagne also has these attributes and, although it can be more moderate in intensity, has engaging acidity and a quite delicious palate.

Food to go with Champagne needs to be elegant, tasty, bold, fresh, clean and, above all, simple. It can be crisp fried as the acidity will cut through and leave your palate refreshed and wanting more!

Australian and other sparkling wines often show less yeast autolysis characters and lack the richness and complexity of French Champagne so the food match can be simpler and lighter.

The recipes in this chapter are mainly tasty morsels that can be served in a precise, sophisticated manner as small bites that can be taken from platters, or they can be served more generously as individual portions in a casual or semi-formal dinner party setting. For example you could easily serve the baccalà croquettes as single-mouthful portions, or you could make them larger and serve them drizzled with a simple caper mayonnaise as a beautiful starter or brunch. You could slice slivers of the sugared cured beef wrapped around grissini, or pile them in loose bundles on plates drizzled with olive oil and crusty, just-baked baguette on the side.

Oysters with pancetta and kaffir lime
23

Garlic fried marron with peach and baby cos salad
and buttermilk dressing
24

Taramasalata and lemon on toasted brioche
27

Pumpkin pithiviers with toasted walnuts
28

Duck liver parfait
31

Baccalà croquettes
32

Sugared cured beef
35

Poached pork cheek with tuna mayonnaise
36

Watermelon with Persian feta and butter-fried sage
38

Tuna carpaccio
41

Oysters with pancetta and kaffir lime

Some flavours are truly meant for each other, and if you like your oysters cooked rather than natural, try them with pancetta and kaffir lime—you will be an instant convert!

On a baking tray, tightly place the oysters.

Turn grill to high.

Slice the pancetta as finely as possible into strips.

Do the same with the fresh kaffir lime leaves.

Divide the pancetta and lime leaf neatly on top of each oyster.

Season each oyster well, and dot with butter.

Place under the hot grill for approximately 5 minutes until pancetta is just crispy, and serve immediately.

Serves 6

24 half oysters
120 g piece of pancetta
2 kaffir lime leaves
(fresh if possible)
salt and pepper
butter

Garlic fried marron with peach and baby cos salad and buttermilk dressing

This is a meal fit for royalty! Succulent, rapidly cooked marron, sun-ripened peaches and the tangy buttermilk dressing are simply perfect with a glass of intensely flavoured vintage Champagne.

Split marron, and clean out the heads.

Heat the oil to 165 °C.

In a bowl, whisk the egg yolk and vinegar together.

While whisking, drizzle in the vegetable oil slowly.

Once all the oil is incorporated, continue whisking and drizzle in the buttermilk.

Season with salt.

The dressing will be runny, the consistency like pouring cream.

Cut the peaches into slices, and place in a bowl with the baby cos.

Add a pinch of sea salt and pepper, drizzle in the buttermilk dressing and toss through.

Fry marron until barely cooked (approximately 1½ minutes), drain and dust well with garlic powder.

To serve, pile the marron onto the salad on a large serving plate.

Serves 6

6 large marron or
12 small marron

2 tsp powdered garlic

oil for frying

250 g baby cos

2 large ripe peaches

25 ml Chardonnay vinegar

140 ml vegetable oil

1 egg yolk

75 ml buttermilk

sea salt

black pepper, freshly cracked

Taramasalata and lemon on toasted brioche

*The salty, lemony, bold flavours of the taramasalata
highlight the yeasty brioche, to create a seamless match
with Champagne.*

Mix flour, yeast and salt in an electric mixer bowl with the beater attached.

Whisk eggs and milk together, then add to bowl and beat the dough for about 4 or 5 minutes.

Soften the butter with caster sugar and add while machine is on slow speed. Beat for 2–3 minutes.

Prove in a warm place for 2 hours, then knock back.

Refrigerate overnight.

Remove from refrigerator, and knead to fit into greased bread tin.

Bake at 200 °C for approximately 20 minutes.

Soak bread in water until softened.

Squeeze out excess water, and mix by hand or in a food processor with tarama and garlic to a paste.

Add lemon juice, and drizzle in olive oil.

Season with pepper.

Toast slices of brioche until lightly golden and crisp.

To serve, generously spread the taramasalata on to brioche and drizzle with a little olive oil.

Serves 6 as a starter

Brioche [1 loaf]

300 g flour

1 tsp dried yeast

½ tsp salt

4 eggs

40 ml milk

150 g butter

15 g caster sugar

Taramasalata

5 thick slices of robust, day-old white bread

100 g of tarama

1 clove garlic, minced

3 tbsp lemon juice

⅔ cup fruity olive oil

pepper to season

Pumpkin pithiviers with toasted walnuts

*Simple and sophisticated. Take the time to make your
own rough puff pastry. The buttery richness coupled with
clean acidity and lingering aftertaste of the Champagne
will leave highly satisfied guests.*

Dice the onion and pumpkin into 5 mm pieces.

In a pan with some olive oil, sweat off the onion for 5 minutes.

Add the pumpkin, and cook until just tender but not too soft.

You may like to finish it in a moderate oven. Cool.

Roll the pastry to a large square.

Cut six circles 8 cm wide, then cut six circles 10 cm wide.

Place some pumpkin mix in centre of the small circle.

Place the large circle on top, and press down to seal the sides.

Brush the pithiviers with egg wash, and bake in 190 °C oven for 12–15
   minutes until golden.

Toast the walnuts in 180 °C oven for 5 minutes.

Rub off any loose skins (it is best to use a clean, dry teatowel, capture the
   nuts in the teatowel and rub vigorously while warm).

Make dressing with balsamic vinegar and extra virgin olive oil.

Toss walnuts and parsley in dressing.

To serve, place in centre of plate, scatter with walnut and parsley dressing.

Serves 6

Pumpkin pithiviers

1 medium pumpkin

1 medium brown onion

olive oil

1 batch rough puff pastry
(see page 204)

egg wash

salt and pepper

Dressing

1 cup picked flat leaf parsley

⅔ cup walnut kernels

30 ml balsamic vinegar

60 ml extra virgin olive oil

Duck liver parfait

*The texture of this parfait is like velvet and
the taste intense, balanced and engaging.
An absolute winner with Champagne.*

Preheat oven to 150 °C, and line a 30 x 8 cm bar tin with cling wrap.

Leave aside.

Place all the reduction ingredients in a pot, and reduce to 50 ml of syrup.

Remove bay leaf and cinnamon stick from syrup—it will be quite thick.

Place half the duck livers in a blender and while it's on, add half the butter,
     half the eggs, half the cream and reduction syrup.

Strain into the lined bar tin, and repeat for the remaining ingredients.

Season with salt, pepper and grated nutmeg while stirring gently in the tin.

Place the tin in a 'water bath' (fill another tin with hot water) and bake for
     30–40 minutes.

The parfait should be just firm when taken out.

Remove from water bath.

Place in refrigerator overnight to set.

Serve with croutons and caramelised onion.

Serves 6 as a starter

500 g duck livers

400 g butter, melted

4 eggs, whisked lightly

50 ml cream

salt and pepper

nutmeg

Reduction ingredients

100 g shallots

10 g thyme

1 cinnamon stick

1 bay leaf

400 ml Port

2 cloves garlic

Baccalà croquettes

Piping hot and well seasoned, these are very inviting with a glass of Champagne. Both the texture and flavour of the crumb and the saltiness of the baccalà (salted cod) seem to really lift the concentration of the palate of Champagne.

Soak the fish overnight in a couple of changes of water to reconstitute it and lower the saltiness.

Drain well, and pat dry with paper towel.

Poach in milk flavoured with bay leaf.

Flake the fish.

Mix in the potatoes while still warm and add the dill and butter.

Form into small shapes about the size of a Champagne cork.

Whisk milk and egg together to make egg wash.

Roll the croquettes in flour, then egg wash, then bread crumbs.

Deep fry until golden, about 4–5 minutes.

Serves 6 as a starter

100 g salted fish
(snapper or cod)

milk

2 bay leaves

500 g royal blue potatoes,
cooked in skins,
then peeled and mashed

2 tsp dill, chopped

1 tsp butter

Crumb

2 cups fresh breadcrumbs

1 egg

1 cup milk

1 cup plain flour

oil for frying

Sugared cured beef

So simple to prepare and so tasty, you will find many ways to serve this beef. It will slice thinly more easily if it is very chilled.

Place the salt, sugar and pepper in a food processor, and blitz to a coarse consistency.

Rub the mixture over the beef, and place in refrigerator.

Turn every 12 hours for 4 days.

Brush excess mixture off the beef.

Slice as thinly as you can.

Serve wrapped around olive grissini or piled on top of a grilled peach.

The cured beef will last up to a week.

Serves 6

500 g piece Scotch fillet
½ cup rock salt
½ cup dark brown sugar
¼ cup whole peppercorns
Olive grissini (see p. 208)

Poached pork cheek with tuna mayonnaise

A very elegant canapé with loads of flavour, this pork can really handle an intense acidic wine. I love to serve a small plate piled with thin slices and drizzled with the mayonnaise.

Slice the shallots and place in a pot with the white wine, stock, sage and peppercorns.

Bring to a boil, and turn down to a simmer.

Place the pork in the liquid, and gently braise for 2 hours.

Remove the pork cheek, and place in the refrigerator.

Whisk the egg yolk with the mustard and lemon juice.

While whisking drizzle olive oil in slowly.

Once all the oil has been incorporated, break up the tuna and fold in.

Season with salt.

To serve, slice the pork cheek thinly, and drizzle the tuna mayonnaise over it.

Scatter some capers over the top.

Serves 6

8 pork cheeks
1 cup white wine
1 litre chicken stock
4 fresh sage leaves
2 shallots
4 peppercorns

Tuna mayonnaise
100 g cooked tuna
3 egg yolks
200 ml olive oil
1 tsp Dijon mustard
3 tbsp lemon juice
salt
baby salted capers, washed and drained

Watermelon with Persian feta and butter-fried sage

The soft, salty feta is a perfect foil for the sweet, crunchy melon. Serve on plates, scattered with the sage and a glass of chilled sparkling red.

Cut the melon into thick slices, then into 2 cm cubes, removing as many seeds as you can.

Place on absorbent paper to soak up as much juice as possible. Chill.

Heat butter or ghee until it begins to foam, then fry sage leaves in batches until they crisp.

Drain on absorbent paper.

Place melon cubes on platter.

Spoon the cheese and oil over the melon cubes in small fragments.

To serve, scatter with sage leaves, and grind some fresh pepper over the top.

Serves 6

1 small ripe watermelon

150 g Persian feta in oil, crumbled, and returned to oil

24 fresh sage leaves

butter or ghee to fry sage

1
CHAMPAGNE

Tuna carpaccio

Blood oranges are the best citrus to serve confidently with Champagne. They are tart but in a gentle, smoother way than regular oranges. The slivers of pickled ginger are most inviting.

Peel and segment oranges, capturing any juice.

Slice each segment into two pieces, again capturing any juice.

Mix the juice with the vinegar and olive oil; season.

Slice the tuna as thinly as possible and lay in a single layer onto plates.

To serve, spoon over the dressing, and scatter the orange segments, coriander and ginger.

Serves 6

800 g fresh sashimi-grade tuna

3 blood oranges

1 tsp Chardonnay vinegar

salt and pepper

3 tsp olive oil

3 tsp picked coriander leaves

1 tsp pickled ginger, cut into slivers

A single mouthful of yeasty, intensely chilled Champagne, a crisp rich parmesan wafer, fresh crabmeat, lemon zest, dill, a touch of cream …

Hand-picking Chardonnay at **Cape Mentelle** Margaret River

Sunset over Cabernet Sauvignon vines **Cape Mentelle's Estate Vineyard** Margaret River

2
LIGHTER WHITES

Lively, sassy and perfectly suited to the tastes of summer.

Aromatic unoaked (and occasionally lightly oaked whites) like Riesling, Semillon, Sauvignon Blanc, Semillon Sauvignon Blanc blends, Pinot Gris and Pinot Grigio and Viognier are as varied as their regions and countries of origin. With lively, zesty acidity, beautiful fruit aromas, sassy palate flavours and punchy clean aftertaste, they cry out for the tastes of summer: seafood, salad and barbecues.

I try to use a light hand when preparing these recipes. By that I mean I tend to be scant rather than generous with seasoning, and keep ingredients cool and the colours and flavours vibrant and true. The crab and green pea is a wonderful taste sensation, much loved over many seasons, and it exemplifies the philosophy of simple, no fuss and careful wine selection when enjoyed with a zesty, limey and youthful Semillon Sauvignon Blanc. Similarly the disarming intensity of Viognier will be truly enhanced by the crusty golden artichoke and potato pavé.

With age some of these wines take on a different flavour as the acidity softens and they become mellow and gain toasty flavours. Then they really enhance foods that have been roasted or seared to caramelise, crisped and crunchy and with sauces thickened with olive oil or butter.

2

LIGHTER WHITES

Crabmeat with green pea
51

Whiting with saffron batter and shaved fennel salad
52

Goats' cheese penne with fresh peas and parmesan crumble
55

Warm potato and speck salad with caper salsa
56

Artichoke and potato pavé
59

Asparagus with crunchy egg
60

Dill and soft herb omelette
63

Seared scallop with ratatouille
64

Tiger prawns with celery salad and lime and ginger dressing
67

Scallops with coconut bisque
68

LIGHTER WHITES

Crabmeat with green pea

The combination of green pea and crabmeat drizzled with some piquant olive oil is a winner, and you can either go posh with your presentation or take it easy and pile the two flavours rustic style on fresh baguette. It's striking with a young zesty Semillon Sauvignon Blanc.

Bring a pot of water to a boil for the peas, add a good pinch of salt and cook the peas for 4 minutes.

Drain the peas, and reserve about half a cup of the water.

While the peas are still warm, add the pecorino and, with a hand blender or fork, crush the peas to a coarse texture, adding a tablespoon of the oil and some of the cooking water.

Season with salt and pepper.

Wrap with cling wrap and place in refrigerator to cool (this is can be done a couple of hours ahead).

In a bowl mix together the crab, lemon zest and juice, the chopped dill and crème fraîche.

Season with salt and pepper.

To serve, make a ring of pea mixture using a egg ring or cutter in the centre of the plate. Portion the crabmeat on top of the pea, and drizzle with olive oil.

Serves 6

200 g cooked crabmeat
zest and juice of 1 lemon
2 tsp crème fraîche
or sour cream
salt and pepper
2 tbsp dill
300 g frozen peas
50 g grated pecorino
extra-virgin olive oil

Whiting with saffron batter and shaved fennel salad

This recipe has youthful Riesling written all over it!
We always mix the batter with a spoon rather than a
whisk to keep it thicker and less airy.

In a large mixing bowl place flour, cornflour, salt and saffron threads.

Make a well in the centre, and add the cold soda water slowly, mixing a smooth batter with the consistency of runny cream. Leave aside.

Wash the fennel well. With a mandolin or knife carefully shave the bulb as finely as possible, and mix together with the garlic, vinegar and olive oil.

In a large saucepan heat some oil to approximately 180 °C.

When hot dredge the whiting fillets in a little flour, then dip into batter and fry until golden brown (approximately 3-4 minutes).

To serve, place a mound of fennel in the centre of a serving plate. Put 2 whiting fillets on top, and serve with lemon wedges.

Serves 6

12 whiting fillets, skin on

a little flour to dust

pinch saffron

50 g flour

100 g cornflour

250 ml cold soda water (approx.)

pinch of salt

oil for frying

2 large fennel bulbs

1 clove garlic, crushed

1 tbsp Chardonnay vinegar

3 tbsp olive oil

lemon wedges to garnish

picked fennel tips to garnish

Goats' cheese penne with fresh peas and parmesan crumble

*The richness of the parmesan crumble really boosts
the appeal of a lemony Riesling.*

Remove crusts and cut bread into chunks and process to a fine texture.

Rub the butter and the flour together until combined.

Add the parmesan and breadcrumbs.

Rub together into pea-sized pieces and place on a baking sheet.

Bake in 180 °C oven for 12 minutes or until golden brown.

Set aside to cool.

Cook the pasta in a large pot of salted water.

Scoop the penne out, then cook the peas for 5 minutes.

Drain peas and crush a third, and fold in the goats' curd and chopped parsley; season to taste.

Toss penne, curd, extra peas, butter and extra-virgin olive oil together.

Season with salt and pepper.

Scatter with parmesan crumb and serve.

Serves 6

Parmesan Crumb

50 grated parmesan

250 g loaf of bread

50 g butter

100 g flour

200 g goats' curd

½ cup parsley

500 g of large penne

500 g fresh peas

salt and pepper

2 tbsp butter

100 ml extra-virgin olive oil

LIGHTER WHITES

Warm potato and speck salad with caper salsa

Try a Viognier or Pinot Gris with this. The speck and capers give lots of vibrant depth of flavour—use Kipflers or a waxy potato to soak up the dressing.

Cut the speck into 1 cm dice, and cut the potatoes into suitable bite-size pieces.

Begin to cook the speck in a baking tray on top of the stove.

As the fat starts to run, add the potatoes, and season with salt and pepper.

Place the tray in the oven and roast until potatoes are tender and speck is well crisped.

In a mixing bowl make a salsa with the pickles, capers, parsley, onion, lemon zest and juice, and pepper.

Drizzle mix with olive oil, and set aside.

To serve, add the warm potatoes and speck to the salsa and mix gently through. Moisten with a little olive oil if required, and serve immediately.

Serves 6

1.5 kg potatoes

300 g speck

olive oil

½ cup diced dill pickles

¼ cup salted baby capers, salt washed off

¼ cup chopped flat-leaf parsley

¼ cup finely diced Spanish onion

zest and juice of 2 lemons; zest to be finely chopped

pinch ground white pepper

2 tbsp extra-virgin olive oil

Artichoke and potato pavé

*This is disarmingly rich, and if you portion then reheat
to crisp the edges, it is most delicious with an intense
aromatic wine like Pinot Gris.*

Peel the potatoes and cut them into slices 2 mm thick using a mandolin
or knife.

Drain the artichokes and slice them thinly.

Toss the potato slices in cream, and season with salt and pepper.

Line a tray 15 cm by 20 cm with baking paper, then place a thin layer of
potatoes on the bottom.

Spread half the artichokes in the tray, then add another layer of potato.

Repeat, then pour the remaining cream on top.

Bake at 180 °C for 40–50 minutes.

Serves 6

1.2 kg royal blue potatoes
150 g marinated artichokes
1½ cup cream
salt and pepper

2
LIGHTER WHITES

Asparagus with crunchy egg

This is sensational with a chilled glass of Sauvignon
Blanc. You do need to be careful handling the eggs,
but the incredible appeal of yolk oozing over crunchy
crumb and the asparagus is definitely worth it!

Soft-poach the eggs, remove from hot water and gently plunge into iced
water immediately to stop the eggs from cooking further, drain.

Carefully dust the eggs in flour, then dip them in the egg wash and coat
in breadcrumbs.

Place on a tray and chill in refrigerator.

When ready to serve heat oil to 165 °C.

Gently lower the eggs into the oil, and fry until golden.

Meanwhile grill or pan-fry asparagus with a little olive oil and salt and
pepper until tender.

To serve, portion asparagus onto serving plates, top with a crunchy egg,
a drizzle of olive oil and serve immediately.

30 spears fresh asparagus

olive oil

salt and pepper

6 eggs

2 cups fresh breadcrumbs

flour and egg wash for crumbing

vegetable oil to deep fry egg

Serves 6

2
LIGHTER WHITES

Dill and soft herb omelette

A glass of chilled young Riesling and a simple,
luscious omelette is a perfect Sunday brunch.

Mix egg gently with shallots and herbs, season.

Brown the breadcrumbs in sizzling butter in a pan, turn the heat down and
    pour in the egg mixture.

Stir gently and sparingly with a fork, bringing the outside edges in.

Roll onto a plate, and serve immediately.

Serves 1

2 eggs

½ shallot, chopped finely

½ tbsp chopped herbs
(dill, parsley, thyme)

1 tbsp fresh breadcrumbs

1 tsp butter

salt and pepper

Seared scallop with ratatouille

The power of the ratatouille and the sumptuousness of the scallops make this a choice for an aged Riesling that is showing toasty, honeyed flavours.

To make the ratatouille chop the eggplant, capsicum, shallots and zucchini as finely as you can.

Sauté the garlic in olive oil, add shallots and thyme, cook until translucent, add tomato juice and reduce by half.

Cook each vegetable separately in a small amount of olive oil until cooked al dente. Season.

Chop olives, and mix all the vegetables together to finish the ratatouille.

Splash some olive oil, salt and pepper on to the scallop meat.

Heat a large frypan or barbecue plate to high.

When the pan is hot, sear the scallop meat on both sides for 1 minute.

To serve, place three circles of warmed ratatouille on a plate and carefully top each with a scallop, and drizzle with a little olive oil.

Serves 6

18 scallops
1 medium eggplant
1 large red capsicum
1 medium zucchini
½ cup pitted kalamata olives
2 cloves garlic, minced
3 shallots
olive oil
salt and pepper
½ cup tomato juice
5 stalks thyme

LIGHTER WHITES

Tiger prawns with celery salad and lime and ginger dressing

*This salad sings out for a straight Sauvignon Blanc,
perhaps with cool, slow barrel-fermentation crafting,
giving it a long, powerful finish.*

Peel and finely slice the ginger and the shallots, and place in a bowl with the juice of the limes and sugar.

Stir to dissolve the sugar, and set aside.

Peel the prawns, leaving tails on.

Wash the fennel and celery.

Slice the fennel finely on a mandolin or with a knife.

With a peeler, peel fine strips from the celery.

Whisk the olive oil into the lime juice, and adjust for seasoning.

Toss the fennel and celery together.

Place the prawns in the salad, and dress with the lime dressing.

Pile into bowls.

To serve, finish with a drizzle of dressing.

Serves 6

24 cooked tiger prawns
6 celery sticks
2 fennel bulbs
3 limes
2 cm piece ginger
1 shallot
2 tsp sugar
¾ cup olive oil
salt and pepper

Scallops with coconut bisque

When we first served this 'bisque' with a lively, just released Semillon Sauvignon Blanc from the Clare Valley, the green peppercorns, coriander and the brandy gave a layer of flavour to the coconut and chicken broth. Make sure you add the scallops at the last minute so that they are barely cooked.

Place the tomato purée, shallots, saffron and brandy in a pot, and simmer for 5 minutes.

Add the chicken stock, and cook for 5 minutes.

Add the coconut milk and cook for 5 minutes.

Season to taste, and add the green peppercorns and coriander.

Blend with a stick blender until smooth.

Reheat to simmering for 1 minute. Season.

Slip the scallop meat and spinach into the simmering bisque, cook for 1 minute and remove from heat and serve immediately.

Serves 6

18 scallops, cut in half
200 g baby spinach leaves
500 ml chicken stock
1 cup tomato purée
1 cup coconut milk
pinch saffron
2 tbsp brandy
1 tsp green peppercorns
salt
½ cup chopped coriander leaves
2 shallots finely sliced

The freshest of fish, grilled perfectly,
spattered with fruity extra-virgin
olive oil, a generous splash of lemon,
baby capers, a scattering of fresh
dill, a chilled Sauvignon Blanc ...

Young Pinot Noir vines, clone 777, at sunrise **Picardy Winery** Pemberton

3
ROBUST WHITES

Robust white wines demand robust food.

Often barrel-fermented, most often barrel-matured, and often Chardonnay, robust white wines demand robust food. Many of us have loved Hunter Valley Semillons and equally aged Riesling, and some barrel-fermented Sauvignon Blancs also fall into this slot. Have the courage to serve intensely crafted food with lots of layers of flavour, and you will be rewarded with a great dining experience.

These recipes need love and passion to bring out the intensity to match the richness of the wines, so be generous with your portions and your seasoning. An extra slurp of olive oil here and there won't go astray.

Techniques such as roasting tomatoes or frying herbs, or using black olives, will give added flavour. Searing to caramelise, as we do with the gnocchi, and reducing the sauce, as with the shiitake on the lobster, are useful ways to build flavour effectively, which when enjoyed with these wines is significantly more satisfying.

With age Chardonnay can become honeyed and toasty while in youth it is often intense, vegetative and long.

Veal schnitzel with panzanella and black olive dressing
79

Yabby with smoked trout and fried dill pasta
80

Grilled swordfish with candied lemon
83

Goats' cheese gnocchi with roasted cherry tomato
and white anchovy dressing
84

Butter poached lobster with shiitake reduction
87

Slow roasted tomato with chèvre
88

Chicken à la minute with eggplant parsley salad
91

Caramelised cauliflower salad with shaved parmesan
92

Onion, olive and thyme puff sticks
95

Roasted turkey breast with green olive and artichoke salsa
96

Veal schnitzel with panzanella and black olives

A rich, crafted, buttery Chardonnay will envelope the savoury flavours of this salad. You could use Japanese-style breadcumbs to give extra crunch to the veal.

Season veal slices and dust with a little flour.

Place each slice in some egg wash and crumb lightly. Set aside.

Rip the bread into walnut size pieces, drizzle with olive oil to moisten, and season. Set aside.

Cut the tomatoes into half, and add to the bread in a large mixing bowl.

Peel onion and, with a mandolin or knife, slice it as finely as possible.

Add to tomatoes. Slice the capsicums into thin slivers, and tear the basil leaves onto all ingredients.

Lastly add finely chopped anchovy fillets, and season well. Gently fold all ingredients through to mix with finely chopped olives and seasoning.

Make a dressing with oil and balsamic and toss through.

In a frypan, gently cook the veal slices. Drain well.

Drizzle with olive oil and a generous splash of balsamic vinegar.

Serve with panzanella on the side.

Serves 6

6 x 120 g thin veal slices
1 cup fresh breadcrumbs
plain flour for dusting
egg wash
salt and pepper
oil to fry
1 red capsicum, roasted, skinned, deseeded
1 yellow capsicum, roasted, skinned, deseeded
1 small loaf of dense, day-old bread
1 punnet cherry tomatoes
3 anchovy fillets
1 small red onion
handful fresh basil leaves
¾ cup pitted kalamata olives
olive oil
balsamic vinegar

Yabby with smoked trout and fried dill pasta

A generous bowl of this pasta and a glass or two of
elegant, barrel-matured Chardonnay or perhaps a
similarly crafted Viognier makes for a splendid lunch.

Crack the shells off the yabbies, devein and cut them in half.

Bring a large pot of salted water to boil for the pasta.

Remove the stems from the dill, and in frypan add ½ cup olive oil.

Heat the pan to medium/high and carefully fry the dill tips until crisp (approximately 1 minute).

Remove dill from pan and drain well on absorbent paper.

Set aside, and reserve oil to add to pasta.

Slice the shallots finely.

Cook the pasta. Be careful not to overcook the angel hair as it is quite delicate.

Drain the pasta, and immediately place it in a large mixing bowl with reserved oil.

Toss together with the yabbies, trout, shallots and fried dill. Season well.

Serves 6

12 small yabbies, cooked

500 g smoked trout, picked from bones

3 shallots

500 g angel hair pasta

extra-virgin olive oil

salt and pepper

2 cups fresh dill

Grilled swordfish with candied lemon

This beautiful candied lemon salad has been on our Margaret River menu for many summers. The sweet sour lemon is an outstanding match for lavish, voluptuous Chardonnays.

Marinate swordfish pieces in olive oil, orange zest and coriander.

Knock marinade off before grilling.

Grill on hot plate for approximately 3 minutes on each side.

Peel lemons with a vegetable peeler, then with a sharp knife slice the peel very finely, lengthways.

In 1 litre of boiling water bring the lemon peel to the boil until rind is tender (approximately 5 minutes). This will remove the bitterness.

Strain, and rinse well under cold running water.

Combine the water with the caster sugar.

Bring to the boil, and place lemon rind in the syrup.

Boil for about 15 minutes, until the lemon is very tender and the syrup has thickened.

Turn off the heat and add currants. Allow to cool.

To serve, mix desired amount of drained lemon candy with equal amount of flat-leaf parsley. Spoon over swordfish pieces.

Serves 6

Swordfish

6 x 150 g pieces swordfish

½ cup chopped coriander leaves

olive oil

zest 2 oranges

Candied lemon salad

4 large lemons

2 cups water

2 cups caster sugar

½ cup currants

flat-leaf parsley

Goats' cheese gnocchi with roasted cherry tomato and white anchovy dressing

This gnocchi and subtle anchovy will bring up all the complexity of an elegant, restrained Chardonnay in the lighter style, still oaky but not obviously so.

Hang the ricotta overnight in muslin to firm.

Crack eggs into a bowl, and gently them break up with a fork.

Add the ricotta and goats' cheese, and gently fold in the parmesan.

Combine the ricotta mixture with the flour to achieve a smooth dough.

Roll out on a well-floured bench and, with a sharp knife, cut into 2 cm squares.

Blanch in simmering salted water for 6 minutes, then drain, and toss in a little olive oil.

These gnocchi can be served immediately or warmed when used later.

Pre-heat the oven to 150 °C.

Slice the cherry tomatoes lengthways, season with salt and pepper, and drizzle with olive oil.

Place in oven for 20–30 minutes.

In a mortar and pestle, grind the anchovy fillets, and slowly add 100 ml of olive oil.

Add 1 tbsp of the brine of the anchovy fillets to the dressing.

Heat a pan, and add a tablespoon of olive oil.

Sauté the gnocchi, then add the tomatoes to heat through.

To serve, place in a serving bowl, and drizzle with anchovy dressing and fried basil.

Gnocchi

250 g goats' cheese

250 g ricotta

3 eggs

¼ cup grated parmesan

¾ cup flour

salt

White anchovy dressing

4 white anchovy fillets

olive oil

salt and pepper

1 punnet cherry tomatoes

fried basil leaves

Serves 6

Butter poached lobster with shiitake reduction

Luxurious, beautiful and truly tasty.
Serve the very best from your cellar.

Place lobster in a large bucket, and immerse in cold water.

Once lobster has drowned, twist the body away from the head.

Take the meat out of the shell (tail).

Place the clarified butter in a pot, and melt until just simmering.

Place the whole lobster tail in the butter, and barely simmer for 15 minutes until just cooked through.

In an open frypan, add a splash of olive oil, shallots and finely sliced mushrooms.

Sauté for 5 minutes on a low heat until mushrooms are tender.

Turn up the heat slightly, and add the vinegar. Reduce by half.

Finally add the cream and salt and pepper.

When the sauce starts to thicken, remove from heat and set aside.

Slice the warm lobster tail on the 'round' (so as to give each guest half a tail).

To serve, divide reduction onto 6 plates, and sprinkle the fresh parsley.

Place warm lobster on top of reduction.

Serves 6

3 live lobster
1 litre clarified butter
(see p. 208)

Shiitake reduction
olive oil
2 shallots, finely chopped
200 g shiitake mushrooms
200 g button or
swiss brown mushrooms
50 ml Chardonnay vinegar
300 ml cream
salt and pepper

¼ cup fresh chopped
flat-leaf parsley

Slow roasted tomato with chèvre

These tomatoes become so intense in flavour when roasted
that they are almost breathtaking. They can handle as
much new, tasty, buttery, oaky Chardonnay as you can find!

Skin the tomatoes, and leave whole.

Slice each clove of garlic into fine slivers, then slice a small cut into each
tomato and push the garlic into flesh.

Sit tomatoes on a wire oven rack on top of an oven tray, season with
salt and pepper, drizzle with olive oil and roast in a 150 °C oven for
2–2½ hours.

Divide tomatoes on to plates, shave chèvre on top, and drizzle with olive oil
and a grind of black pepper.

Serves 6

12 Roma vine-ripened tomatoes
olive oil
2 large cloves garlic
salt and pepper
300 g mature chèvre

Chicken à la minute with eggplant parsley salad

The harissa and eggplant add punch and weight that really lift the chicken. A Pinot Gris with a couple of years bottle age, or a barrel-fermented Semillon would be a great companion.

Slice the chicken in half to create six thin pieces.

Season, and leave aside.

Cut the eggplant into 1 cm dice, and sprinkle with cooking salt.

Leave for 30 minutes.

Wash, drain and dry eggplant well. In a bowl add eggplant, crushed garlic, olive oil, rind of lemon and harissa paste.

Marinate for 30 minutes.

On a barbecue plate or in a hot pan, cook eggplant quickly, tossing through heat for approximately 10 minutes until soft and cooked through.

When slightly cooled toss with parsley and gently stir through.

Using the same hot plate or pan, sear the chicken steaks and cook on each side for 1–2 minutes. Season.

To serve, place chicken in the centre of a plate, and add the eggplant and a squeeze of lemon.

Serves 6

6 chicken breasts
½ cup olive oil
salt and pepper
1 large eggplant
2 cloves garlic
2 cups roughly picked
flat-leaf parsley leaves
juice and rind of
1 medium lemon
½ tsp harissa paste

Caramelised cauliflower salad with shaved parmesan

This is a great way to lift the intensity of flavour of a
relatively subtle vegetable. Caramelising the cauliflower
and being liberal with shaved parmesan creates the
richness to handle a bolder, more intense wine.

Cut the cauliflower into bite-size flowerets.

In a pot of boiling salted water blanch the cauliflower pieces, and remove
when just tender (approximately 5 minutes).

Refresh them in iced water and set aside.

In a hot pan, heat olive oil and add the flowerets and brown sugar and roll in
pan until it just starts to caramelise or finish in a very hot oven.

Place on a serving plate, and top with shaved parmesan and fried shallots.

Serves 6 as a side dish

1 small cauliflower

4 tsp olive oil

2 tsp brown sugar

salt and pepper

½ cup parmesan, shaved

½ cup fried shallots (available
from Asian groceries)

Onion, olive and thyme puff sticks

These are yummy—you can never make enough!
The recipe for rough puff pastry is on page 204.

Roll pastry to ½ cm thickness on a floured board.

In a food processor add olives, fresh thyme leaves and a little olive oil.

Pulse until you have a smooth paste.

Carefully spread onto pastry as thinly as possible.

Slice red onions finely, and lay over pastry.

With a sharp knife cut pastry into 12 narrow strips.

Starting with the first cut piece, roll neatly and twist each piece as you finish.

Repeat with remaining strips.

Lay each strip on a lined baking tray and bake in a 180 °C oven for approximately 10 minutes until golden.

Serve immediately!

Serves 6 as an appetiser

1 batch rough puff pastry

2 medium red onions

olive oil

¾ cup pitted kalamata olives

4 sprigs thyme

salt and pepper

ROBUST WHITES

Roasted turkey breast with green olive and artichoke salsa

*This meal, with its massive flavour from the spice rub,
rich succulent meat and a complex salsa, demands a
fantastic Chardonnay.*

Crush the peppercorns and juniper and mix with the olive oil, thyme and salt.

Rub the turkey flesh with this mixture, under the skin and all over.

Place the turkey on a baking tray, cover it with aluminium foil and cook it in a 140 °C oven for 45 minutes.

Remove aluminium foil and return the tray to the oven at 180 °C for a further 30 minutes.

Cover and let rest for 15 minutes.

Place all salsa ingredients in a mixing bowl and mix together.

Set aside in refrigerator for at least 1 hour for flavours to infuse.

To serve, slice turkey thickly, spoon salsa over the meat and drizzle with a little extra olive oil.

Serves 6

Turkey

1 turkey Kiev
(approximately 1 kg)

6 juniper berries

1 tsp Schezwan peppercorns

6 stalks fresh thyme

2 tsp salt

¼ cup olive oil

**Green olive and
artichoke salsa**

2 cup preserved artichokes,
roughly chopped

200 g pitted green olives,
roughly chopped

3 tbsp chopped dill

1 tbsp baby capers

2 tbsp Cabernet vinegar

4 tbsp olive oil

1 tsp brown sugar

salt and pepper

Aromatic ripe peach, cut and grilled to caramelise the flesh; fine, butter-like, nutty prosciutto; a drizzle of salsa verde; barely oaked, elegant, restrained Chardonnay …

Tendrils left on trellis wire, Semillon vines **Cape Mentelle** Margaret River

Chardonnay vines and olive grove **Picardy Winery** Pemberton

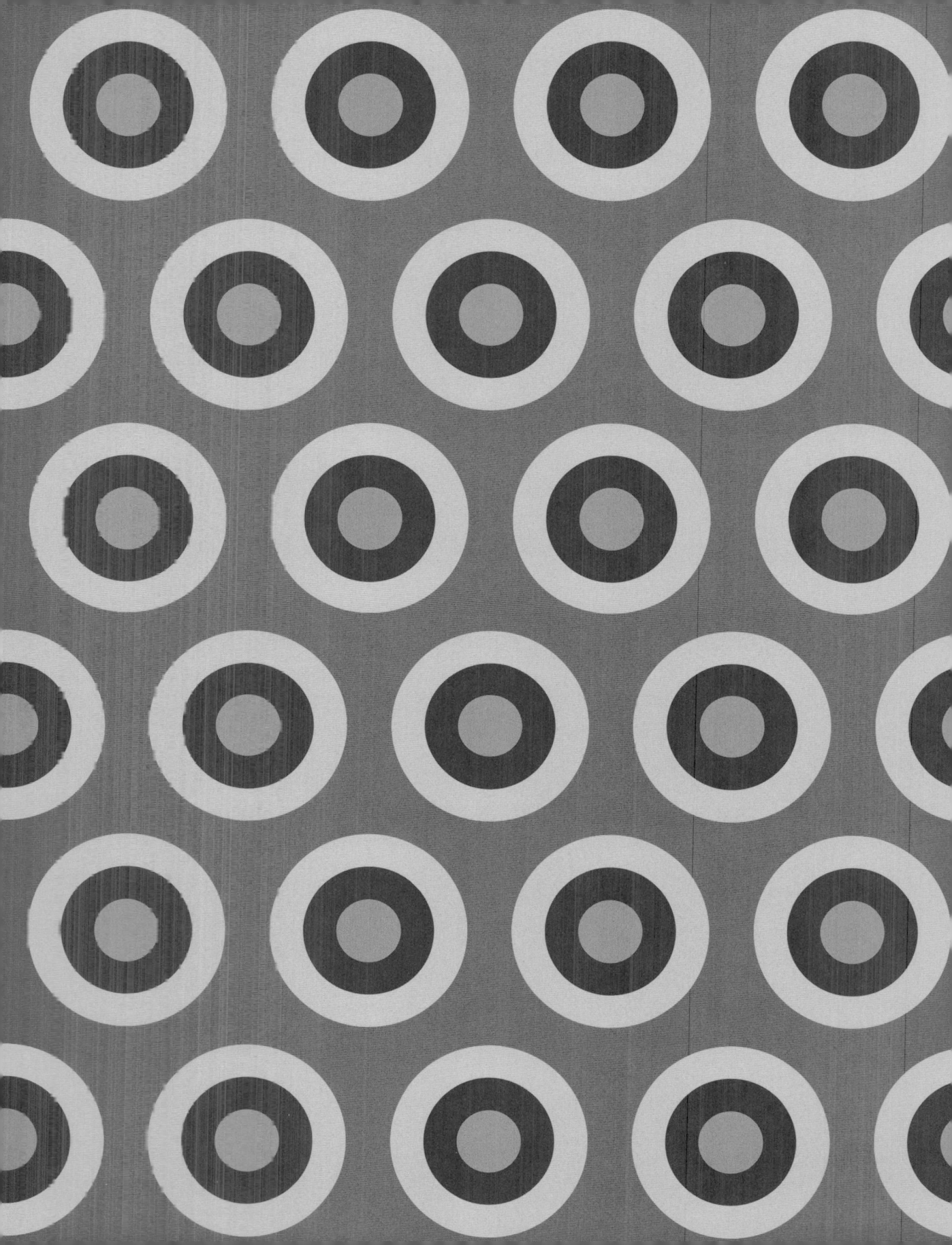

4
LIGHTER REDS

Their spiciness, ripeness and juiciness suit our lifestyle.

As consumers we have been happily inundated in recent times with new styles and varieties of light red wines. Australians have embraced Sangiovese, Tempranillo, Grenache–Shiraz–Mourvèdre blends and Shiraz–Viognier blends, and eagerly look to what the Italians and Spanish are producing and sending to our shores. It seems to me we are enjoying the 'weight' of these wines: their spiciness, ripeness and juiciness suit our lifestyle and climate and much of the way we like to eat in terms of simple, fresh and increasingly regional food.

The finished texture of some of the meals in this chapter can also contribute to their enjoyment. A crisped pork belly, for example, has much more appeal and flavour than otherwise; similarly by using freshly made, coarse breadcrumbs rather than finely ground ones you will add a delicious buttery crunch to the chicken tenderloins.

Another useful technique is to build flavour in sauces. You will see in the snapper mornay that by making fish stock to add to the basic béchamel you will create a whole extra dimension in an otherwise fairly plain sauce. The further addition of smoky paprika really makes a simple dish very powerful.

The food in this chapter of all the chapters in this book is the most versatile. If you love the ideas and embrace the philosophy of matching flavours you will be rewarded with enormous pleasure. A generous hand in preparation can almost tip this food into the more robust red category, yet a meek touch could bring a recipe back to being a great white wine companion.

103

Lamb cutlets with caramelised pumpkin and feta salad

The feta and pumpkin add both a lightness and a density to this meal, creating an opportunity to match a spicy, lighter red style albeit with some sturdy tannin to go head to head with the feta.

Quarter the onions, roast them with olive oil and seasoning, and allow to cool.

Peel pumpkin and cut it into 3 cm chunks.

Toss in oil, season and place on roasting tray.

Roast it in a moderate oven until tender and starting to take on a golden, 'caramelised' colour.

Cool but do not chill—this is most delicious if the other ingredients of the salad are mixed through the warm pumpkin.

Gently mix olives, capers, feta, dill, onions, chickpeas and vinegar together with the pumpkin.

Drizzle the lamb cutlets with olive oil and season, then seal them on each side for approximately 4 minutes.

Remove from heat and rest them for another 5 minutes.

To serve, simply pile the lamb cutlets on top of the pumpkin salad and serve immediately.

Serves 6

18 lamb cutlets

2 kg pumpkin

olive oil to cook

salt and pepper

3 medium red onions

1 cup pitted large green olives, chopped coarsely

2 tsp baby capers

1 cup soft feta, preferably one stored in oil

3 tsp chopped dill

400 g cooked chickpeas

2 tsp balsamic vinegar

Pork belly with apple and muscatels

It is both the succulence of the pork and the clean acidity of the apples that make this dish so complete. A light-style red with some gentle oak and intense fruit such as a Grenache or Shiraz–Viognier would definitely fit the bill.

The first job is to braise the pork belly.

This takes time and can be done the day before.

Place the pork into a deep tray, add stock and cover, and slowly cook in the oven at 150 °C for about 3 hours.

Once finished, remove from the oven, then press the meat down between two trays, placing some weights on top to press the belly down.

Place in the refrigerator for a couple of hours or overnight until you are ready to portion.

In a mixing bowl slice the apples (skin on) as finely as possible.

Cut the muscatels in half, and add to apples.

Season with salt and pepper, and add the lemon juice to mix. Set aside.

Portion the pork into six pieces, and brush some honey on the skin.

Place in a hot oven (about 220 °C) to crisp the skin.

To serve, remove pork (once it is crisp) from the oven, place onto a serving plate and top with apple salad.

Serves 6

600 g pork belly

2–3 litres chicken stock

honey to brush

2 large Golden Delicious apples

200 g muscatels (taken from cluster, seeds removed)

juice of ½ lemon

LIGHTER REDS

Sardine tapenade

It's ideal to leave the tapenade coarse and have 'bits' of sardine and olive.
Spread it on garlic rubbed toasts—these flavours really complement the spicy tones
of the red blends such as Grenache–Shiraz–Mourvèdre, Tempranillo and Sangiovese.
A terrific, casual appetiser.

Drain the sardines, and place in a food processor with the
remaining ingredients.
Pulse the food processor and drizzle in the olive oil to moisten the paste.

Serves 6 as an appetiser

300 g sardines
1 cup pitted kalamata olives
zest and juice of 1 lemon
2 tsp toasted pine nuts
1 tsp baby capers
2 tsp chopped parsley
olive oil

Quail with pomegranate couscous

This dish has punchy flavour, and the couscous is very clean and fresh. Rosy, lighter-style reds would be perfect.

In a pan, dry-fry or roast sumac and salt until aromatic.

Rub the spice mixture and roughly torn sage leaves into the quail, and leave for a couple of hours.

Drizzle with olive oil, and grill or barbecue.

Heat stock and add to couscous in a large bowl. Stir, cover and rest for 20 minutes.

Break up couscous with a fork.

Split pomegranate and gently remove seeds, discard skin.

Add pomegranate to couscous with dill and parsley.

Make a dressing with vinegar and olive oil and then dress the couscous.

Place couscous on a plate and serve with quail.

Serves 6

Quail

12 deboned quail

1 tsp sumac

1 tsp sea salt

4 fresh sage leaves

olive oil

Pomegranate couscous

500 g couscous

500 ml chicken stock

1 pomegranate

½ cup picked dill

¼ cup picked parsley

150 ml extra-virgin olive oil

LIGHTER REDS

Chicken tenderloins with fresh crumb, parsley and parmesan

Such a favourite! Loved by everyone, this recipe is so
simple to make. A medium-weight Shiraz with more
spice and less chocolatey oak would be a terrific match
and lots of green salad to balance the richness.

Remove sinew from tenderloin.

In a bowl mix breadcrumbs, parsley, parmesan, herbs and salt and pepper.

Place the butter in a large bowl, and add all the tenderloins.

Allow to sit for approximately 1 minute in the butter before removing one by one and generously patting the crumb mixture onto the chicken pieces.

Tightly lay on a greased baking tray.

Drizzle on any remaining butter, and bake in a moderate oven for approximately 10–15 minutes until the crumb begins to brown and crisp and chicken is cooked.

18 chicken tenderloins

150 g butter, melted

2½ cups coarsely ground fresh breadcrumbs

½ cup coarsely chopped flat-leaf parsley

½ cup grated parmesan

salt and pepper

Serves 6

Slow-cooked ocean trout with Jerusalem artichoke purée and crisp peas

The artichoke purée takes this fish from being a white wine partner to that of a medium-weight red. The crisp peas also give an extra dimension that pairs with an elegant cool-climate Cabernet Sauvignon.

Peel the artichoke and potato, and cut to the same size.

Place in a pot, and add water to cover.

Add some salt, and cook until soft.

Place the potato and artichokes in a blender, and blend until smooth, adding a little cream. Season to taste.

Heat oil in a deep pan to 180 °C.

In a mixing bowl combine flours, and stir in the beer to make a runny batter.

Drop peas in the batter, scoop out with a slotted spoon and fry in the hot oil (about 1–2 minutes). Drain on absorbent paper.

Divide the fish into 150 g portions, brush with olive oil and season.

In an oven preheated to 120 °C, cook the fish for 20 minutes.

The fish should just yield to the touch.

To serve, place the artichoke purée in centre of the plate and ocean trout on top, and garnish with crisp peas.

Serves 6

Jerusalem artichoke purée
500 g Jerusalem artichoke
1 large potato
salt and pepper
cream if needed

Crisp peas
oil for deep frying
50 g rice flour
100 g plain flour
beer (approx. 375 ml)
150 g peas

900 g ocean trout
olive oil

Salmon en croute

This is so impressive! Ideally serve the salmon whole and cut it at the table. Pinot Noir and a green salad is all it needs.

In a mixing bowl add sliced mushrooms, fresh thyme, dill, salt and pepper. Sauté gently with butter.

Roll pastry out onto a floured bench until it is 2 cm thick and large enough to encase the salmon. Brush with melted butter, lay the salmon fillet on the pastry and carefully spread the mushroom mixture on top. You may like to tuck the tail and sides under the fillet to give an even thickness.

Fold pastry over the salmon and press the edges together to seal.

Brush the pastry log with egg wash.

Place on a baking tray and put into a hot oven (about 180 °C) until golden brown.

For the beurre blanc, reduce in a pot the wine, vinegar and the bay leaf. Add the cream and keep reducing until large bubbles start forming in the pot.

Take it off the heat and whisk in the cold butter, a little at a time.

Once all the butter is whisked in, adjust the seasoning, and keep in a warm area until you serve it.

Be careful not to reheat this sauce or it will split.

To serve, cut the salmon into six pieces and drizzle with beurre blanc.

Serves 6

Salmon en croute

1.2 kg side of skinless salmon

1 batch of puff pastry

100 g melted butter

salt and pepper

handful fresh thyme, finely chopped

handful fresh dill, finely chopped

200 g field mushrooms, finely sliced

1 tbsp butter

egg wash

Beurre blanc

2 tbsp white vinegar

1 bay leaf

2 tbsp white wine

100 ml cream

150 g butter, cold and diced

Barbecued squid with anchovy crumb

The flavour and crumbs and using a barbecue turn this normally white wine companion into a red wine champion!

Clean the squid by pulling out the head and any debris.

Wash out the tube, and set it aside. Clean the tentacles.

In a food processor combine the breadcrumbs, parsley, lemon zest and anchovy, and process to combine, add in a drizzle of olive oil.

Stuff the squid tubes with the breadcrumbs mixture and push the tentacles into tube.

On a hot barbecue cook the squid for 8 minutes turning frequently until just cooked and tender.

Season and squeeze over lemon to serve.

Serves 6

12 local whole squid
2 cups fresh breadcrumbs
1 tbsp lemon zest
½ cup parsley
4 anchovy fillets
½ cup olive oil

LIGHTER REDS

Snapper mornay with smoky paprika

This recipe is a great example of how to intensify flavour. Big fish stock and smoky paprika, a potentially mild sauce, becomes powerful and flavourful—turning a traditional white wine meal into a red wine bonanza!

Using a lidded shallow pan large enough to hold fish in a single layer, add wine, lemon juice, salt, peppercorns, herbs and bay leaves, and bring to simmering point.

Add fish and enough water to almost cover fish.

Place lid on pan and simmer gently 3–5 minutes, depending on thickness of fish.

Turn off heat, and allow fish to cool in liquid for at least half an hour.

Remove fish, flake and place into six ramekins (approximately 12 cm).

Fish should be a snug fit.

Strain poaching liquid and reduce to ¾ cup.

Melt 60 g of butter until frothy, add flour, and cook 1–2 minutes without browning.

Add milk, stock and wine, stirring continuously until boiling and thickened.

Add paprika, lemon juice, seasoning and ½ cup of cheese.

Stir until cheese has melted.

Check for seasoning before pouring over fish evenly in ramekins.

Sprinkle over breadcrumbs and remaining cheese, and dot with extra butter.

Place in hot oven or under grill until sauce is bubbling and the top browned.

Serve immediately with crusty bread.

Serves 6

Snapper

750 g snapper fillets

1 cup dry white wine

juice of 1 lemon

1 tsp salt

10 whole peppercorns

1 cup chopped parsley, fennel and thyme

3 bay leaves

water

Velouté sauce

60 g butter

60 g plain flour

1 cup milk

¾ cup fish stock (reduction)

¼ cup dry white wine

½ tsp smoky paprika

salt and pepper to taste

juice of 1 lemon

1 cup grated tasty cheese

¼ cup fresh breadcrumbs

extra butter

Figs and goats' curd with Vincotto

The sweetness of the figs, the richness of the goats' curd and the piquancy of the Vincotto make for a complexity that really holds up with a young Pinot Noir.

Cut figs in half, grill or barbecue until cut side is just caramelised.

Portion figs out onto plates.

Divide curd evenly onto figs and drizzle with extra-virgin olive oil and vincotto.

Season and garnish with dill and parsley.

Serves 6

9 medium-sized fresh figs

300 g fresh goats' curd

olive oil

salt and pepper

2 tbsp Vincotto

½ cup picked dill and parsley

Succulent roasted turkey, pancetta stuffing moist with feta and roasted peppers, mellowing, aromatic, strawberry-textured Pinot Noir ...

Plunging at Moss Wood Wilyabrup

Overlooking Shiraz vines at the picturesque **Willow Bridge Estate** in the majestic Ferguson Valley

5
ROBUST REDS

This chapter to me, says winter...

I feel as if we grew up with these wines: Barossa, Coonawarra, Hunter Valley, Margaret River. Rich, oak-integrated, ripe fruit, intense alcohol and dedicated craftsmanship have given us wines we love to drink. These wines insist on robust flavours, often meat and often braised or roasted. However, as we do look to eat lighter by using the method of cooking to influence the final taste, you can use poultry and seafood as the base ingredients and create flavour intensity to match these fabulous wines.

This chapter says winter. Spending a rainy afternoon preparing, filling the house with comfort aromatics—this food is for taking time over the eating, letting the conversations linger long after the meal is over.

When braising ensure that you take time. A braised beef cheek can't be hurried. The resulting sauce, whether it be from the lamb necks or venison osso bucco, will be a genuine delight, packed with the mingling flavours from well-cooked vegetables, fresh herbs, red wine, stock and of course the meat itself.

5
ROBUST REDS

Hand-cut pasta with lamb neck braise
134

Beef cheek with salsa verde
137

Venison osso bucco with juniper and bay pies
138

Roasted spatchcock with olive and avocado salsa
141

Rib eye with prosciutto, red wine and prunes
142

Baked prawns with eggplant and roasted pepper salad
145

Wild mushroom tart
146

5
ROBUST REDS

Hand-cut pasta with lamb neck braise

This recipe is everything wonderful about braising. Leaving you with a moist delicious sauce, the lamb is rich, satisfying and intense. Bring on that gutsy Shiraz you have in your cellar!

Brown lamb neck pieces, and season.

Remove lamb and set aside.

Sauté the onion, garlic, celery and carrot until they begin to colour.

Return lamb to the pan, and deglaze with the red wine.

When red wine has reduced by half, add the tomato purée, stock to cover lamb, and bay leaf and thyme.

Cover with a tight-fitting lid, braise for 2 hours at 150 °C, then remove lid and continue to braise for another half-hour.

Add olives and parsley, stir through and allow to cool slightly.

When cool shred the meat, discarding the bones. Set the meat aside.

Mix pasta ingredients until dough comes together. Place dough on bench and knead until smooth.

Put through a pasta machine on a fine setting. Setting number 5 is recommended. Cut into roughly shaped strips.

Bring a pot of water to the boil, and cook strips in batches for 3–5 minutes per batch. Drain, and oil well. Set aside.

To serve, add the meat to a large pan heated to medium and enough of the sauce to cover. When just heated through, add pasta and toss together. Spoon into bowls, and serve immediately, scattered with picked parsley.

Serves 6

Braised lamb necks

1.5 kg lamb necks

1 large brown onion

6 cloves garlic

1 medium carrot

1 stalk celery

1 litre chicken stock

1 cup tomato purée

200 g kalamata olives

¼ cup parsley, chopped

5 stalks thyme

1 bay leaf

1 cup red wine

parsley to serve

salt and pepper

Pasta dough

375 g plain flour

4 egg yolks

2 whole eggs

1 tsp salt

1 tsp water

5
ROBUST REDS

Beef cheek with salsa verde

*The freshness of the salsa verde brightens the intensity
of the braised meat, which is quite unctuous and serious.
A cool-climate Cabernet Sauvignon with blackberry
tones would be perfect.*

Ensure your butcher has removed sinew from the beef cheeks.

Chop the vegetables, then place the beef, vegetables, garlic, herbs, pancetta
and wine together and marinate for at least 12 hours.

Take beef out of the marinade. In a little olive oil, brown in a casserole dish
or baking pan big enough to hold the ingredients.

Add the marinade to the meat and bring to the boil.

Add the beef stock, turn down and simmer or braise in oven for
approximately 4 hours.

The beef cheeks should be tender and almost fall apart.

Process the salsa ingredients together in a food processor or, for a smooth
sauce, blitz in a blender.

Serve beef cheeks drizzled with salsa verde, mashed potato and extra sauce.

Serves 6

Braised beef cheeks

2 kg beef cheeks
4 medium carrots
2 medium brown onions
4 cloves garlic
6 stalks fresh thyme
2 bay leaves
4 sticks celery
80 g of pancetta, cut into 4
2 cups red wine
4 litres beef stock
olive oil to brown

Salsa verde [makes 1 cup]

2 cloves of garlic
2 anchovy fillets
½ tbsp capers
salt
½ tsp pepper
1 cup fresh basil leaves
½ cup flat-leaf parsley
1 bunch chives
40 ml red wine vinegar
200 ml olive oil
preserved rind of ¼ lemon

5

ROBUST REDS

Venison osso bucco with juniper and bay pies

Red wine! Red wine! Red wine! These pies are absolutely delicious. A Shiraz, preferably with lots of American oak maturation, will be so perfect here.

Coat the osso bucco in the seasoned flour, and seal until golden brown on both sides in a well-oiled pan.

Place these into a braising pan, and add the chopped vegetables, crushed tomatoes, white wine, herbs, spices and anchovy fillets if desired.

Top up with the beef stock until the meat is covered.

Cover with baking paper, then aluminium foil.

Place in the preheated oven (160 °C) and cook for 3–4 hours until meat is very tender.

When cool, remove all meat from the bone, add some of the sauce to make a moistened pie filling and leave aside.

Roll pastry. From an edge cut suitable sized pie lids. Using remaining pastry, cut and line muffin-size tins.

Fill the pies with filling until about three-quarters full.

Turn in any pastry overflow and then top the pies with the pre-cut lids and brush with egg wash.

Bake in a 180 °C oven until pastry is golden (approximately 15 minutes).

Serves 6

1 kg venison osso bucco

1 cup seasoned flour
(flour mixed with a pinch each
of paprika, sea salt, white
pepper, turmeric and cumin)

1 cup white wine

1 x 440 g tin crushed tomatoes

1 small carrot, roughly chopped

1 stalk celery, roughly chopped

1 medium onion, peeled and
roughly chopped

2 bay leaves

10 black peppercorns

5 juniper berries

2 stalks each of
rosemary and thyme

2 anchovy fillets (optional)

beef stock

olive oil

1 batch puff pastry
(use recipe on p. 204)

egg wash

5
ROBUST REDS

Roasted spatchcock with olive and avocado salsa

By adding raisins to the tapenade you create a natural sweetness that mingles with the caramelised flavours of the roasted bird. Cabernet with a touch of vanillin French oak will be a wonderful match. The raisin tapenade recipe is on page 209.

Rub the spatchcocks with salt and pepper and olive oil.

Slice the lemons thinly, and place inside the cavity of each bird and a piece or two between the skin and the meat.

Place birds on a rack on an oven tray and roast in a moderate oven for 45 minutes until golden and just starting to fall from the bone.

When cooked, rest in a warm place and baste with any pan juices.

Meanwhile put together the salsa by mixing the avocado with the raisin tapenade and parsley and moisten with extra olive oil. Season.

Serve the birds whole with boiled potatoes and a generous dollop of salsa.

Serves 6

Roasted spatchcock

6 spatchcock

2 lemons

salt and pepper

olive oil to cook

Salsa

2 ripe avocados, cut into chunks

1 cup coarse raisin tapenade
(see recipe on p 209)

½ cup picked
Italian parsley leaves

2 tbsp olive oil

5
ROBUST REDS

Rib eye with prosciutto, red wine and prunes

This sauce is sweet, savoury and dense all at once.
By serving this sauce with veal rather than beef the
dish will not be overpowering, rather a gentle, natural
companion to an aged red wine, particularly a Shiraz.

In a hot pan seal the seasoned racks with a little olive oil.

Place the racks in an oven pan and cook in a 180 ºC oven for
30–40 minutes.

Take out of oven, remove from the pan and wrap in aluminium foil.
Leave aside.

Return the pan to stove top, and deglaze with red wine and Port.

Place tomatoes, prosciutto and prunes in the pan.

Simmer to reduce.

Turn stove top to low, then carefully and quickly whisk in cold butter.

Slice racks and serve with sauce.

Serves 6

2 veal racks with
6 chops in each

olive oil

salt and pepper

2 large Roma tomatoes, skinned,
deseeded, chopped finely

10 prunes, cut in half

6 slices of prosciutto,
cut in half lengthways

¼ cup red wine

½ cup Port

100 g cold butter

5
ROBUST REDS

Baked prawns with eggplant and roasted pepper salad

Once again eggplant works to add robustness both texturally and in terms of flavour. With its companion ingredients it allows the prawns to be enhanced by a big ripe red rather than to be swamped by it.

Slice the eggplant lengthways into 12 slices.

Sprinkle with salt and set aside for 30 minutes.

Wash, drain and dry.

In a hot oiled pan, fry lightly on both sides until soft.

When cool to touch, carefully wrap each prawn in eggplant and tuck edges together to make neat. Leave aside in refrigerator.

On a tray, lightly oil the whole capsicums and roast in a 180 °C oven for approximately 20 minutes or until skin blisters.

Remove and cool slightly.

Remove skin and seeds from capsicum, and chop into small dice.

In a large bowl, whisk together oil, lemon juice, harissa and cumin.

Add tomatoes, capsicum, garlic, parsley and season to taste.

On a baking tray place eggplant wrapped prawns and bake in a 180 °C oven for approximately 10 minutes.

Remove from oven.

Spoon peppers mix into bowls and top with prawns.

Serve immediately.

Serves 6

12 banana prawns, peeled and deveined

2 medium eggplants

olive oil

3 medium tomatoes, peeled and deseeded

2 red capsicum

2 garlic cloves minced

1 tsp ground cumin

½ tsp harissa

½ cup olive oil

juice of 1 lemon

½ cup parsley, chopped

salt and pepper

5
ROBUST REDS

Wild mushroom tart

Dense, earthy and flavourful the mushrooms will pair with
an intense, ripe, youthful Shiraz. A spinach salad with
some shaved parmesan will be the perfect accompaniment.

Chop the butter into the combined flours and seasoning to achieve a
breadcrumb-like mixture.

Mix the egg and yolk into the flour until all is combined, wrap and place in
the refrigerator to let it rest for at least 1 hour.

Take out the pastry and roll it out to fit a 25 cm tart pan, then blind bake at
180 °C until golden brown.

Remove from oven and let the base cool.

Sauté onions in butter with bay leaf and thyme, cook until soft and golden
add mushrooms and cook until tender.

Then add drained and sliced porcini, and cook for a further 2 minutes.
Allow to cool.

Mix eggs, egg yolk, cream and seasoning together.

Place porcini mix in the tart case and cover with egg mix.

Cook at 160 °C for 20-25 minutes until just set.

Serve warm

Serves 6

Pastry

315 g plain flour

170g butter

1 tsp cornflour

1 egg

1 egg yolk

salt and pepper

Filling

2 medium onions,
finely sliced

50 g butter

3 stalks thyme

1 bay leaf

100 g dried porcini, soaked in
warm water and sliced

4 large field mushrooms

300 g swiss brown mushrooms

5 eggs

1 egg yolk

200 ml cream

salt and pepper

Fragrant spice-rubbed
venison loin, seared,
rested, rosemary-roasted
shallots, dusty, cedary,
cassis-aged Cabernet Sauvignon....

Old growth Semillon vines at **Amberley** Margaret River

6
DESSERT WINES

A truly great way to finish a meal.

From ethereal French Sauternes to perfumed German Riesling, the fabulous Australian botrytis Semillon styles and our intensely unique fortified Muscats and Tokays, the savoury liquorish Portuguese Ports, dessert wines are truly a great way to finish a meal—with dessert, of course!

Whether you choose to make an intense, dense and sweet, wobbly crème caramel, or a generous bowl of trifle brimming with the perfumed, moist and textured tastes, or the beautifully viscous semifreddo with a creamy, velvety mouthfeel and studded with enriched fig, remember that it can be tricky matching sweet with sweet, so err on the side of caution. Sometimes less is more.

6
DESSERT WINES

Vanilla sponge roll with soft cocoa centre
157

Treacle cigars
158

Pear pie with walnut pastry
161

Turkish delight meringue
162

White chocolate and cardamom mousse
165

Passionfruit curd cake
166

Crème caramel
169

Tempura strawberries with crema catalana
170

Savoy trifle
173

Dried fig semifreddo
177

6

DESSERT WINES

Vanilla sponge roll with soft cocoa centre

Although you may think cocoa lacks the oomph of chocolate, it has a lovely soft texture and an almost savoury flavour. A slice of this sponge roll is quite delicious with a dollop of cream and a glass of Tawny Port.

Soak the gelatin sheets in cold water for 15 minutes.

Combine the cream and water, and bring to a boil.

Drain the gelatin sheets, and add to the cream mix with the cocoa and sugar.

Stir to dissolve the gelatin, and cook for further 5 minutes.

Let cool and place in refrigerator for 2 hours.

Separate the eggs, then cream the yolks with half the sugar and the vanilla bean, and set aside.

Whip the whites with the remaining sugar to soft peaks, and fold into the yolks.

Sift the flour, then fold it into the egg mix.

Line a tray 40 cm by 25 cm with baking paper, and spread the sponge mixture evenly.

Bake at 190 °C for 5–7 minutes.

Turn sponge out on to lightly sugared greaseproof paper under which a well-rung-out, just damp tea towel has been placed.

When the sponge has cooled, place on a clean tea towel or sheet of baking paper and spread the cream over half the sponge.

Spread the cocoa on the remaining part and roll it up, using the tea towel as a guide.

To serve, slice and serve with cream.

4 eggs

125 g sugar

125 g flour

1 vanilla pod

250 ml whipping cream

250 ml water

15 gelatin sheets

125 g Dutch cocoa

250 g sugar

1 cup whipped cream

Serves 6

6
DESSERT WINES

Treacle cigars

*These are so good! So simple and so great
with a glass of botrytis Semillon.*

Place walnuts, breadcrumbs, brown sugar, treacle and lemon zest in food processor and pulse to combine.

Take one sheet of filo and brush with butter.

Fold it in half and brush edges with butter.

Place some mixture in the middle and roll into a cigar shape.

Brush with butter and place on baking sheet.

Repeat for 11 more. Scatter some of the walnut mixture on top and bake at 200 °C for 12–15 minutes.

Serves 6

12 sheets filo pastry
2 cups walnuts
½ cup brown sugar
¼ cup treacle
1 cup fresh breadcrumbs
zest of 1 lemon
1 cup melted butter

6
DESSERT WINES

Pear pie with walnut pastry

*I first tried this dessert with a glass of French Sauternes,
truly a magnificent combination.*

In food processor place flour, cinnamon, sugar and walnuts, and combine.

Add butter and process until mixture resembles breadcrumbs.

Lightly beat egg, vanilla and Madeira, add to dry ingredients and process only until a dough is formed.

Wrap dough in cling wrap and refrigerate for half an hour.

Remove dough from refrigerator and divide off a third of it.

Knead remaining two-thirds and carefully roll a circle large enough to line a sponge tin 20–24 cm x 4 cm high, leaving an overhang of about 5 mm. (If the dough breaks just press it together.)

For the pie top, knead and roll the remaining third of the dough to a circle slightly bigger than the tin's diameter.

Cut an 8 cm circle out of the middle.

Peel and quarter the pears.

Pat dry and arrange neatly on base of pie with narrow ends towards centre.

Slight overlapping may occur in order to fit.

Using a rolling pin, lay top over pears with cut-out circle in the centre of the pie.

Press edges together with small fork and cut away excess dough.

Moisten pie top by brushing with water, then sprinkle generously with sugar.

Bake in centre of 180 °C oven for 40–45 minutes.

Leave to cool in tin for 15 minutes before turning out.

Pile whipped cream in centre of pie and serve.

250 g plain flour
2 tsp ground cinnamon
120 g caster sugar
60 g roughly chopped walnuts
150 g cold unsalted butter, cut into small pieces
1 egg
1 tsp vanilla
1 tsp Madeira
3 medium firm pears
extra caster sugar

Serves 6

6
DESSERT WINES

Turkish delight meringue

The rosewater and slivers of Turkish delight turn a
simple meringue into a masterpiece. The sweetness is of
such intensity that a glass of liqueur Muscat is ideal.

In a large mixing bowl whisk egg whites until stiff.

Add three-quarters of the sugar, the cornflour, vinegar, rosewater and hot
water, and continue to whisk until glossy and thick.

Add remaining sugar slowly.

Fold in Turkish delight pieces and scoop into six greased 8 cm metal rings or
make large quenelle shapes.

Bake in a 150 ºC oven for 10 minutes, then turn oven to 130 ºC and bake
for a further 50 minutes.

Serve dusted with icing sugar.

Serves 6

4 egg whites

150 g caster sugar

100 g Turkish delight,
cut into small pieces

1 tsp rosewater

2 tsp hot water

2 tsp vinegar

2 tsp cornflour

6
DESSERT WINES

White chocolate and cardamom mousse

By infusing the milk with cardamom you create an almost 'savoury' perfume and flavour that keeps the chocolate influence less sweet. This mousse is lovely with a late harvest-style white or German Spätlese style. The white chocolate should be the best you can find.

Crack the cardamom pods and remove the seeds.

With a mortar and pestle lightly crush them, then add these and the bay leaves to the milk.

Heat the milk without boiling it and set it aside.

Gently melt the chocolate.

Whip the cream to medium stage—into soft mounds, not too stiff.

Beat the egg whites to a firm peak with the sugar. Do not overbeat.

When the chocolate has melted pour the milk through a sieve into the chocolate.

Stir together until velvety.

Fold the chocolate mix into the egg whites, then fold in the whipped cream.

Pour or spoon into dishes and chill for 4 hours until set.

Dust with cocoa and caster sugar, and serve.

Serves 6

8 cardamom pods
100 ml milk
3 bay leaves
250 g white chocolate
300 ml double cream
3 egg whites
1 tsp caster sugar

6

DESSERT WINES

Passionfruit curd cake

I think we have made literally hundreds and hundreds of these cakes. They are moist, dense and rich. A botrytis Riesling would be perfect.

Cream the butter, sugar and lemon zest.

Beat in the eggs one by one.

Add softened marzipan in small thumbnail-sized pieces while beating slowly.

Sift together the flour and baking powder, and fold into the egg mixture.

Pour into greased, lined 26 cm cake tin and cook at 180 °C for 50-60 minutes. Cool.

Mix all breadcrumb ingredients to form a rough crumb (you can pulse them quickly in a food processor).

Shake the mixture onto a baking tray and cook for approximately 10 minutes in a 170 °C oven until just becoming golden.

For the passionfruit curd filling, melt butter and sugar together in the top of a double saucepan. This will take about 15 minutes.

On a medium heat whisk in eggs and passionfruit, stirring constantly until mixture starts to thicken (approximately 15 minutes). Do not overheat. Once the mixture starts to coat the back of the spoon, remove from heat. Cool and refrigerate.

When cake is cool, cut through centre to make two rounds.

Spread half the passionfruit curd on bottom half of cake and place the other on top.

Use the remaining curd to drizzle over the top of the cake.

To finish, scatter the crumb on top, slice and serve with cream.

Serves 6

Cake

300 g butter

300 g sugar

300 g marzipan, softened

zest of 1 lemon

8 eggs

200 g flour

1 tsp baking powder

Shortbread crumb

85 g melted butter

75 g sugar

150 g plain flour

35 g almond meal

Passionfruit curd

110 g unsalted butter

230 g caster sugar

90 ml passionfruit pulp

2 large eggs, beaten

6
DESSERT WINES

Crème caramel

A classic dessert, so simple. A 'sticky white' with age will be heavenly with this.

Place sugar and water in a pot.	**Caramel**
Stir to dissolve sugar, and cook on medium to a dark caramel.	¾ cup sugar
Place a tablespoon of water in the caramel, standing back to avoid splatter.	100 ml water
Pour into six 150 ml dariole moulds.	

Crème

Place cream, milk and scraped vanilla bean in a pot and bring to a boil. · 500 ml cream

In a separate bowl, combine egg yolks, whole eggs and sugar, and stir to combine. · 200 ml milk

Pour the hot milk into the eggs, stirring slowly. · 1 vanilla bean

Cover and set aside for 30 minutes. · 5 egg yolks

Strain and pour into the dariole moulds. · 2 eggs

Place on tray and bake at 100 °C. Check after 1 hour. They should be just set. · ¾ cup sugar

If not set, cook for further 10 minutes.

Place in refrigerator for 4 hours.

To serve run a knife around the edge and turn out.

Serves 6

6
DESSERT WINES

Tempura strawberries with crema catalana

These strawberries are amazing, like hot strawberry jam!
A liqueur Tokay will work with both the strawberries and
the toffee and intense creaminess of the crema catalana.

Simmer milk, cinnamon, lemon rind and vanilla beans.

In a bowl whisk egg yolks and cornflour and pour in the hot milk.

Strain and return to a low heat and cook until mixture thickens.

Pour into six ceramic moulds, and place in refrigerator for 6 hours to set.

To make tempura batter, combine the flour and the soda water to get a
pouring cream consistency.

Heat the oil to 170 °C.

Wash and dry the strawberries, dip into the batter and fry for 2–3 minutes.

Drain on absorbent paper.

Sprinkle the crema catalana with antillaise sugar and burn to caramel with
mini kitchen blow torch.

To serve, place on a plate with the strawberries dusted in icing sugar.

Serves 6

Crema catalana
1 cinnamon stick
rind of 1 lemon
beans of 1 vanilla pod
4 egg yolks
50 g cornflour
2 cups milk
½ cup antillaise sugar

Tempura mix
50 g flour
soda water

oil for frying
12 large ripe strawberries
icing sugar for dusting

6
DESSERT WINES

Savoy trifle

Old-fashioned! I'm all for a glass of rose Champagne with this trifle. The lightness of the sponge, the sweetness and richness of the cream will be the perfect foil for it.

Grease Swiss roll tin (approximately 34 x 24 cm), line with greaseproof paper, then grease the paper.

Beat the eggs until frothy, then gradually add the sugar, beating well after each addition. Continue beating eggs and sugar until very thick—this will take 8–10 minutes.

Carefully fold in sifted flour, finally adding hot water and vanilla.

Pour into prepared tin and spread evenly, ensuring that corners are well filled. Bake in a hot oven (210–220 °C) for 8–10 minutes, until pale golden and springy to the touch.

Turn sponge out on to lightly sugared greaseproof paper under which a well-rung-out, just damp tea towel has been placed.

Remove tin and paper, and trim edges from the sponge on all sides.

Make a shallow cut about 1 cm from the nearest side.

Spread warm redcurrant jelly over sponge.

Make a crease at the shallow cut by folding the edge of sponge over to make the inside turn of the roll. Continue to roll sponge using sugared paper and tea towel to make a firm roll. Hold for 1 minute before placing on wire rack to cool, making sure the join is underneath. Leave to cool completely before slicing thinly for the trifle lining.

Continued over page

Redcurrant jelly roll
3 eggs
120 g caster sugar
120 g self-raising flour
2 tsp hot water
½ tsp vanilla
½ cup redcurrant jelly

6
DESSERT WINES

Savoy trifle

Continued

Separate the eggs, add sugar to the egg yolks and beat until light and fluffy.

Strain gelatin and whisk in the hot milk.

Stir over gentle heat until the custard coats the back of a wooden spoon, then allow to cool.

Beat egg whites until very stiff, and whip the cream.

Stir custard over ice until it begins to set.

Fold in the beaten egg whites and whipped cream until well combined.

In a glass serving bowl line the bottom and sides with thin slices of jelly roll, and sprinkle liberally with rum. Fill bowl with cream. Cover top of bowl with more jelly roll slices, again sprinkling generously with rum.

Chill for at least 4 hours before serving.

Serves 6

Cream filling

4 eggs

½ cup caster sugar

1½ cups milk, heated

1 tsp powdered gelatin

1½ cups whipping cream

rum

extra whipped cream to decorate

6
DESSERT WINES

Dried fig semifreddo

You need to drizzle a liqueur Muscat onto this semifreddo as well as drink with it in this instance. For me the dish embodies a childhood memory of an absolutely special treat.

In a mixing bowl place figs, then add brandy and mix.

Heat cream, beat egg yolks and sugar together, and gradually whisk in hot cream.

Stir over gentle heat until the mixture is thick (coats back of wooden spoon).

Add the mixture to the figs and brandy, then cool to room temperature.

Freeze in a metal bowl until almost set.

Beat until mixture doubles in size.

Cover and refreeze in a rectangular mould.

Simmer sugar and water until sugar has dissolved.

Add the figs and cook for 20 minutes. Cool.

Cover outside of the mould with a warm tea towel to release semifreddo onto a platter.

Serve drizzled with liqueur Muscat and baby figs.

Serves 6

Semifreddo
1 cup dried figs, chopped finely
3 tsp brandy
900 ml cream
5 egg yolks
¾ cup caster sugar

Baby figs
18 baby dried figs,
1 cup sugar
1 cup water

An indulgent, dense dollop of chocolate mousse, complex, plummy lingering vintage Port …

Moss Wood Cabernet Sauvignon in barrel, Wilyabrup

Cabernet Sauvignon vines along the dam, Pedestal Vineyard **Larry Cherubino Wines** Margaret River

7
MENUS

The task of taking time and planning a shared meal is for many of us a genuine pleasure. Whether you have saved special wines, been waiting patiently for new season-asparagus or the first truffles, have reason to celebrate a birthday, a special visitor or simply want to have some friends over to enjoy companionship, giving thought to which food with which wine can be great fun and often create congenial and animated debate.

The following menus provide a basis for ideas. For me they provide balance, highlight fresh ingredients and should show your choice of wines in the most food enhanced way. Of course you will use your own interpretation of flavour and style, and finetune the intensity to suit your occasion.

7
MENUS

Shiraz vines in autumn shades **Vasse Felix** Margaret River

MENUS

Casual autumn lunch

Winter is on the horizon, there is a chill in the evening air and finally, the salad season is over. Barebecue the squid and be generous in your spicing of the bisque. Be both cautious and confident as you add the scallops absolutely at the last minute. The chicken is quick and easy and the eggplant offers substance in both texture and flavour. Be bold with a gutsy young spicy red and pull out an aged sweet white with the cake.

Squid with anchovy crumb
Scallops with coconut bisque
Chicken à la minute, eggplant and parsley salad
Passionfruit curd cake

7
MENUS

Winter dinner

Braised beef cheeks, aged sturdy, powerful Cabernet and rain on the roof. Heaven for some! Start the meal with some warmed oysters, the kaffir lime and pancetta offer subtlety and you could venture to a sparkling wine with a generous Pinot Noir component to kick off the evening. The crisped velvety pillows of gnocchi deserve a companion wine with structure, length and complexity. Seek out a bottle-developed white. Decant aged red and pour generously to serve with the unctuous meat. A slither of pear pie, a glass of Sauternes and an evening complete.

Oysters with pancetta and kaffir lime
Goats' cheese gnocchi
Beef cheeks, salsa verde and mash
Pear pie

MENUS

Celebration!

This is a serious menu; you will need to invest time to purchase perfect ingredients and spend some time in the kitchen pulling it all together. Don't be perturbed, the results will be fantastic and delicious. You need an excellent glass of Champagne to start, and follow up with more at the table with the tuna. Invest in a great bottle of Chardonnay or a barrel and bottle–maturated Semillon to serve with the lobster. Choose a cedary, restrained, classic Cabernet Sauvignon with persistent tannins and bold texture and with the rib eye you will have a most fulfilling occasion. Serve a glass of the very best liqueur Muscat with the crisp yet gooey meringue. Dinner at its absolute best!

Tuna carpaccio
Butter poached lobster
Rib eye with potato and artichoke pave and green salad
Turkish delight meringue

7
MENUS

Welcome to spring

I'm suggesting four courses because welcoming spring after the endurance of a cold winter calls for a celebration. The starter and dessert have spring written all over them and depending on your time and mood you may favour salmon with a rich buttery Chardonnay or lamb with a peppery cool-climate Shiraz. Start with a zesty new vintage Sauvignon Blanc and finish with a botrytis style Semillon or Riesling. If you are in for the long haul of four courses (maybe not so difficult to handle!) then try serving the salmon with an aged Riesling and then move to a Cabernet with some silky tannins and a few years' age.

Asparagus with crunchy egg

Salmon en croute

Hand-cut pasta, lamb neck braise

Tempura strawberries with crema catalana

Shiraz at harvest **Lamont's** Swan Valley

7
MENUS

Summer feast

Family get-togethers, friends visiting from afar and the sheer pleasure of the summer break...
Food needs to be easy to pull together, fresh and have a sense of summer. It should
celebrate the season, the heat which ripens fruit and be visually inviting as well as
taste fabulous. Consider serving icy cold Rosé, chill down your lighter style reds and
have some fruity Semillon Sauvignon Blanc on hand. All of these recipes will platter
beautifully to feed many and the swordfish will barbecue effortlessly. Make many more
treacle cigars than you think you need; one of them with a glass of aged vintage Port
and you will probably need two per guest!

Figs with goats' curd and Vincotto
Tiger prawns with celery salad and lime and ginger
Watermelon, feta and sage
Potato and speck salad
Swordfish with candied lemon
Treacle cigars

MENUS

Drinks party

These recipes can be served as finger food, on small plates with baby forks or piled on crusty bread, rustic or sophisticated depending on your mood. You may like to wrap the beef around slices of peach, serve the olive puffs hot from the oven piled high on a wooden board, you could make the pies as small as a couple of bites or larger and present as fork food. I love to serve the crab and pea, layered on small plates, drizzled with some feisty olive oil and a generous amount of dill. Guests love dessert and try making these crème caramels in small dariole moulds, just three or four mouthfuls…arguably irresistible! Serve the best champagne you can afford, chilled, and have a medium-weight white and red on hand, perhaps a Pinot Gris or lightly oaked Chardonnay and a lively Pinot Noir, a spicy Sangiovese or robust Tempranillo. A bottle or two of aged red is probably good to have in reserve and you may like to wrap up with a small taste of aged Muscat with the crème caramels.

Sugared cured beef

Baccalà croquettes

Crabmeat with green pea

Venison osso bucco and bay pies

Onion, olive and thyme puffs

Chicken tenderloins with fresh crumb, parsley and parmesan

Crème caramels

Cabernet Sauvignon in crusher **Lamont's** Margaret River

Cabernet Sauvignon vines at **Leeuwin Estate Vineyard** Margaret River

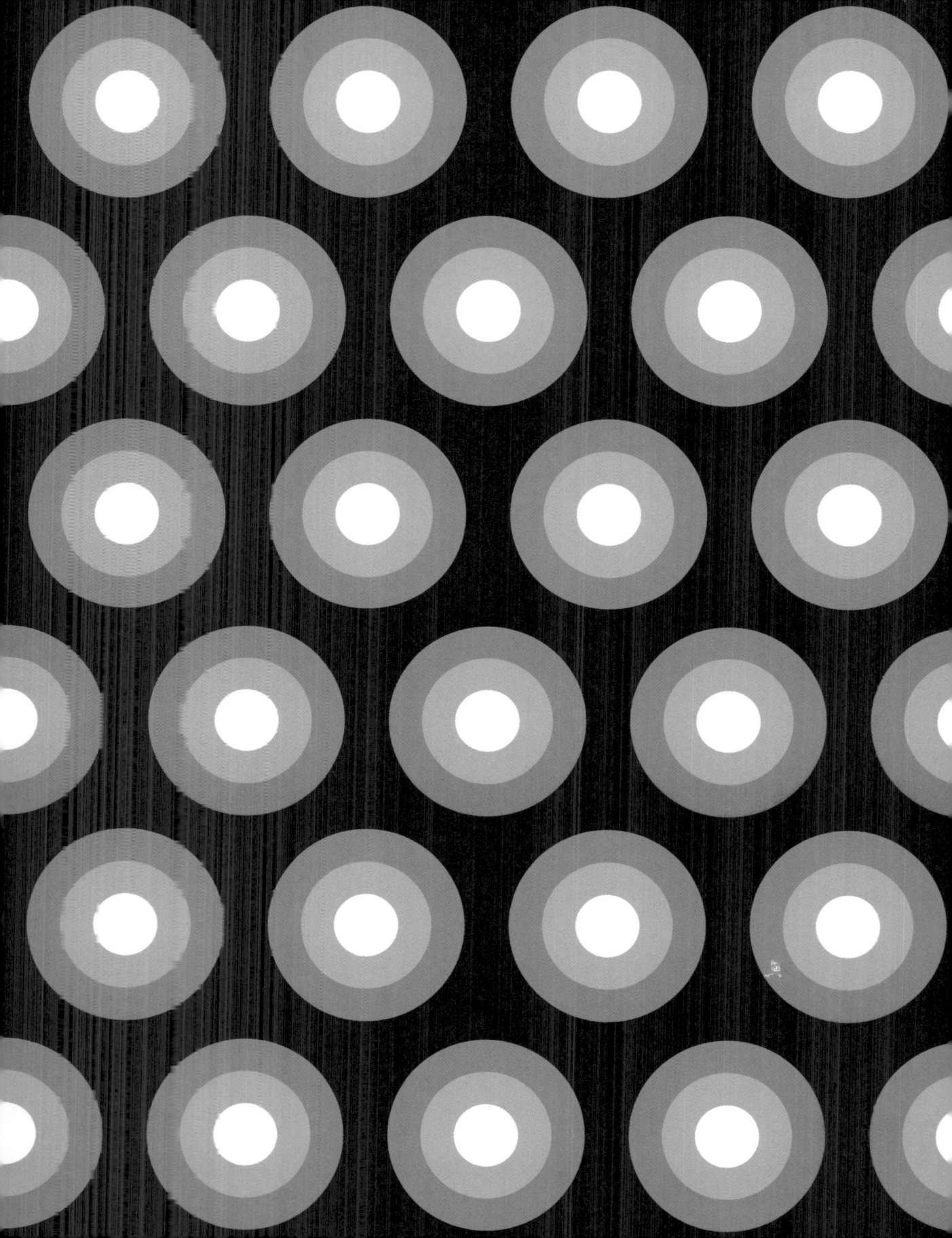

8
BASICS

Quick rough puff pastry

Chill the flour and butter before using.

Chop butter into the flour until pieces are the size of a thumbnail.

Add water and lemon juice, and mix gently

As best you can, press the mixture together into a rectangular shape. There will be chunks of butter showing.

Sprinkle extra flour onto the workbench, and roll the pastry into a long rectangle, 1cm thick. Don't worry if the edges are a little ragged.

Fold the ends in to meet in the centre, then fold together. This will make four layers. This is your 'first turn'.

Turn the piece of dough away from you a quarter of a turn and roll again to form a long rectangle, 1 cm thick. Repeat the folding process. This is your 'second turn'.

Turn the piece of dough away from you a quarter of a turn and roll again to form another long rectangle. This time fold the pastry in thirds as you would a letter, cover it and chill for an hour before use.

The pastry will keep for a couple of days in the refrigerator or in the freezer for a month.

Makes 450 g

½ cup flour
pinch of salt
180 g butter
2 tsp lemon juice
¼ cup iced water

Beef stock

Preheat oven to 180 °C.

Roughly chop vegetables into 1 cm dice.

In a large baking tray, spread vegetables and place bones on top.

Dollop tomato paste onto each bone.

Bake in the oven until brown and vegetables are soft.

Remove bones and vegetables from the baking tray and place in large stock pot.

Meanwhile place the baking tray on top of the stove and turn heat to medium.

Add the red wine and deglaze, scraping any meaty bits that may be left in the pan.

When reduced by half, carefully pour the pan juices over the bones.

Add all the remaining ingredients to the bones.

Top with cold water until completely covered.

Bring the stock to the boil, skim the surface, then reduce to a simmer for approximately 4½ hours.

Remove bones and the bulk of the vegetables from the stock and any scum that may be on the surface.

Carefully pour the remaining liquid into a strainer.

Keeps for 4–5 days in the refrigerator, or frozen for up to a month.

Makes 2 litres

2 kg meaty beef bones

½ cup tomato paste

2 carrots

1 large brown onion

1 stick celery

4 large garlic cloves

2 bay leaves

10 peppercorns

1 cup red wine

5 litres water

Chicken stock

Preheat oven to 180 °C.

Roughly chop vegetables into 1 cm dice.

Roast carcasses and vegetables in a baking tray with olive oil until browned and vegetables are soft.

Tip into stockpot.

Place the baking tray on top of stove and add wine.

Reduce the wine by half over a medium heat.

Scrape any meat and vegetables from the bottom of the baking tray, and add them and the reduced wine to the stockpot with the herbs and peppercorns.

Cover with cold water and bring to boil. Skim the surface regularly.

At boiling point turn heat down and simmer for 2-3 hours.

Strain, and discard the vegetables and carcasses. Allow to cool.

Keeps for 2-3 days in the refrigerator, or frozen for up to a month.

Makes 2 litres

1 kg chicken carcasses

2 carrots

1 celery stick

1 brown onion

4 large garlic cloves

¼ cup olive oil

1 cup white wine

6 peppercorns

10 parsley stalks

6 fresh thyme stalks

3 litres water

Fish stock

Roughly chop vegetables into 1 cm dice.

In a large stockpot, sauté vegetables in oil for 10 minutes over low heat.

Add fish carcasses, parsley stalks, peppercorns and lemon rind, and turn heat to high.

Add white wine and reduce for a couple of minutes.

Cover with cold water and bring to the boil. Skim the surface regularly.

At boiling point, turn heat down and simmer gently for 30 minutes.

Strain and discard vegetables and fish. Allow to cool.

Keeps for 2–3 days in the refrigerator, or frozen for up to a month.

Makes 2 litres

1½ kg whole fish carcasses
(gills and eyes removed)
2 carrots
1 celery stick
1 brown onion
4 large garlic cloves
¼ cup olive oil
6 parsley stalks
6 peppercorns
slice lemon rind
1 cup white wine
3 litres water

Clarifying salted butter

Olive grissini

500 g salted butter

5 g fresh yeast

pinch salt

pinch flour

pinch sugar

2 tsp water

250 g cups bread flour

125 ml water

2 tsp finely chopped
kalamata olives, mixed
to a coarse paste

sea salt

1 tbsp olive oil

In a large saucepan heat butter gently until simmering. The milk solids will fall to the bottom.

Cool slightly, then carefully pour the liquid through a fine strainer to separate from solids. Avoid tipping the milk solids. Discard milk solids.

Place clarified butter in container, refrigerate and use as required.

Mix the yeast, pinch of salt, flour, sugar and water together. Set aside for 10 minutes.

Place the flour in a bowl. Add the yeast mixture and water, and mix together. Knead for 5 minutes.

Cover the bowl and place in warm area for 45 minutes.

Roll the dough out to 25 cm by 20 cm, spread the olive paste over it, and cut into 1 cm strips.

Transfer to a baking tray and cover with cling wrap for 20 minutes, then remove cling wrap.

Drizzle with olive oil and sea salt, and bake at 190 °C for 15 minutes.

Makes 40

Raisin tapenade

100 g pitted kalamata olives
100 g raisins
3 anchovy fillets (optional)
¼ cup picked parsley leaves
1 clove of garlic
3–4 tbsp extra-virgin olive oil
ground black pepper to season

Soak raisins in hot water for 10 minutes to soften, then strain.

Add all ingredients to food processor and pulse until coarsely ground. Season with pepper to taste.

For a coarser tapenade you can hand-chop the ingredients then stir through the olive oil.

Makes 2 cups

Olive tapenade

2 tsp minced garlic
150 g pitted kalamata olives
3 anchovy fillets
2 tbsp red wine vinegar
2 tbsp chopped parsley
1 tbsp capers
4 tbsp olive oil

Pulse all ingredients together in a food processor, or chop and mix together until smooth.

Makes 2 cups

Floral, perfumed,
jewel-like Rosé,
crunchy, salty oyster fritters,
dense garlicky mayo ...

Shiraz fermenting on skins at vintage **Goundry Wines** Great Southern

ACKNOWLEDGEMENTS

Lucky for me, my husband, my family, my colleagues
– Nathan in particular – my staff, my customers,
Frances Andrijich and the people at UWAP have the
passion, enthusiasm and the love for delicious wine and
food in the same way that I do.

Working together on a book, especially one that tries to fit
every 'last bit' between the pages is sometimes arduous,
sometimes hilarious and nearly always exhilarating.

Thanks, all of you.

Kate Lamont.

Seared tuna, just-plucked beans,
vine-sweet baby tomatoes,
a shaving of piquant pecorino,
garlicky, limey olive oil, rich buttery
powerful aged Chardonnay …

Autumn Sauvignon Blanc vines at **Cullen Wines** Margaret River

UWAP is an imprint of UWA Publishing,
a division of The University of Western Australia.

THE UNIVERSITY OF
WESTERN AUSTRALIA
Achieving International Excellence

Published in 2009 by UWA Publishing
Crawley Western Australia 6009
www.uwap.uwa.edu.au

ISBN 9781921401336 (hbk)

A full CIP record for this book is available from the National
Library of Australia.

Printed by 1010 Printing International Limited.
Photographic artwork & CMYK color conversion
by Henrik Tived.

The Publishers would like to thank the following people
for their support. Country Road, Remedy and Table Culture.
Liz McLeod, Catharine Lumby, Robin and Kerry Leen.

The Photographer would like to thank the following people
for their support. Henrik Tived, Maureen and Dan Chadwick,
Kylie Clarke, Vanya Cullen, Clarence Dent, Jacinta Dimase,
Ali Drake-Brockman, Rachel Hobley, Nichola Holgate,
Fiona Hoy, Saviour Kabunda, Alexandra Kemp, Fiona Lamont,
Victoria Laurie, Jennifer Leen, Laity Lencioni, Ma Cuisine –
Cottesloe, Anna Maley-Fadgyas, Rebecca Mansell, Susan
Maushart, Gary Marsh, Michael Muntz, Verity Perna,
Shenae Reilly, Emma Smith, Chloe Stevenson, Mike and
Beth Townsend, Annalise Todd, Mikhaila Todd, Scott Voek,
Kate McLeod, Terri-ann White and Kate Lamont.

INDEX

Voyager Estate Vineyards nestled in the picturesque Stevens Valley area of Margaret River.

Crisped rosewater meringue,
sugar-sweetened raspberries,
lashings of cream, sips of sticky
liqueur Muscat …

Cabernet Tasting at **Cape Mentelle** Margaret River

Juniper and fresh thyme braised beef, a hint of blood orange encased in golden crisped flaky pastry, funky, edgy, ripe cool-climate Cabernet Sauvignon …

Early morning in Cabernet patch **Lamont's** Swan Valley

licious

Artich

borough

Caber

a LAM

ecialist wine S

ood Orange M

e Bar Tus